Helping Your Students With Homework

A Guide for Teachers

By Nancy Paulu

Edited by Linda B. Darby
Illustrated by Margaret Scott

Office of Educational Research and Improvement
U.S. Department of Education

U.S. Department of Education
Richard W. Riley
Secretary

Office of Educational Research and Improvement
Ricky T. Takai
Acting Assistant Secretary

Office of Reform Assistance and Dissemination
Peirce Hammond
Director

Media and Information Services
Cynthia Hearn Dorfman
Director

Reprinted August 1999

For sale by the U.S. Government Printing Office
Superintendent of Documents, Mail Stop: SSOP, Washington, DC 20402-9328
ISBN 0-16-049436-2

Foreword

Homework practices vary widely. Some teachers make brilliant assignments that combine learning and pleasure. Others use homework as a routine to provide students with additional practice on important activities. And, unfortunately, some assign "busywork" that harms the educational process, by turning students off—not only making them feel that learning is not enjoyable or worthwhile, but that their teachers do not understand or care about them.

Homework has long been a mainstay of American education for good reason: it extends time available for learning, and children who spend more time on homework, on average, do better in school. So how can teachers ease homework headaches?

The ideas in this booklet are based on solid educational research. The information comes from a broad range of top-notch, experienced teachers. As you read through, you will find some familiar ideas, but may also find tips and assignments that suit your teaching needs and style.

Students, teachers, and parents or caregivers all play vital roles in the homework process. I challenge you to contribute all you can to making homework meaningful and beneficial for your students.

Peirce Hammond
Director
Office of Reform Assistance and Dissemination

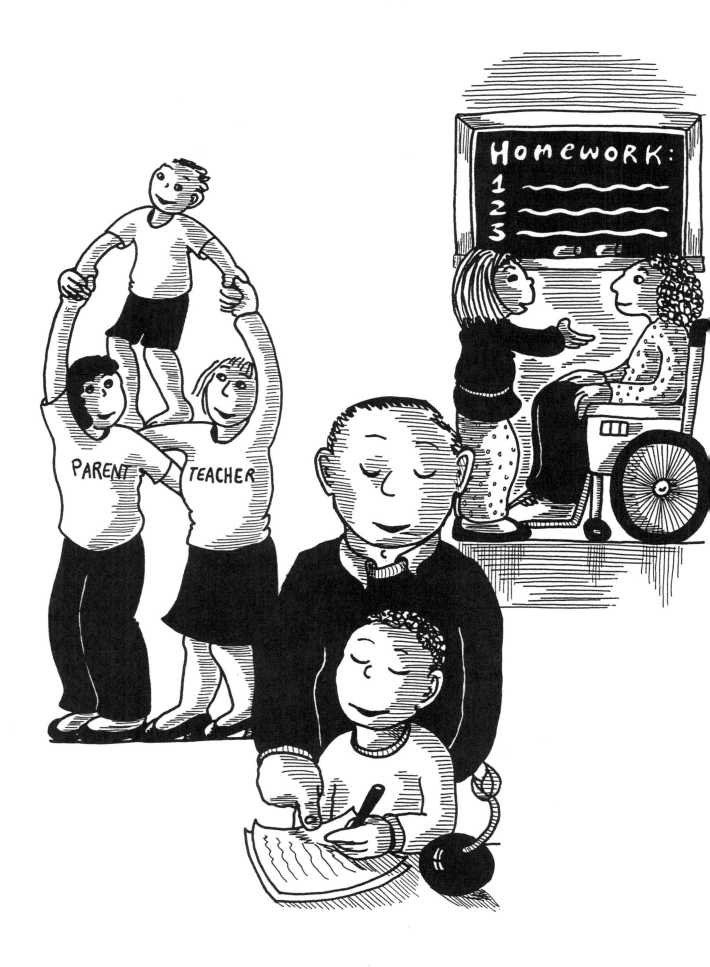

Contents

Homework: A Concern for Teachers

"Homework," says Eleanor Dasenbrook, a sixth-grade social studies and reading teacher in Virginia, "is one of the biggest challenges and concerns I continue to face after more than two decades of teaching."

For many teachers, homework is a major source of angst.

- At a Colorado teachers' workshop, participants discuss how to develop homework that helps children learn and competes with Nintendo.

- At a Texas teachers' meeting, participants address concerns about a lack of parent support for homework.

- In the hallway of a California high school, two teachers debate how to motivate students to complete their homework.

- In a New York teacher's lounge, one occupant talks about the math assignment that her fourth-grade student's dog allegedly chewed to shreds.

The challenges of homework facing teachers today are all the more troublesome given the importance of meaningful and appropriate assignments. Student achievement rises significantly when teachers regularly assign homework and students conscientiously do it, and the academic benefits increase as children move into the upper grades. Homework can help children develop good habits and attitudes. It can teach children self-discipline and responsibility. More importantly, it can encourage a love of learning.

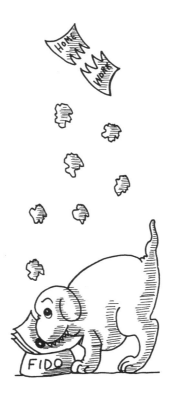

Hurdles to Homework

Homework problems often reflect our changing American society. "Most children don't come home to a plate of cookies and Mom saying, 'Do your homework,'" explains Mary Beth Blegen, Teacher in Residence at the U.S. Department of Education and a veteran Minnesota high school history, humanities, and writing teacher. Many parents report returning home around dinnertime after a hectic day at work, too tired to monitor assignments. Students' personal difficulties and competing priorities can also create obstacles to completing homework successfully.

- Ms. Dasenbrook calls home if students regularly fail to complete assignments successfully. She often learns that parents and caregivers are not aware that a problem exists. "Parents often want their children to do homework shortly after arriving home," she explains. "This is especially true if the parent is still at work because it's a productive way for the children to spend time before mom or dad gets home." But Ms. Dasenbrook knows from experience that children with homework problems usually need to be supervised and held accountable for their work in order to complete it successfully. "I've heard the story many times," she laments. " 'When I get home from work, my child tells me that the homework is finished.' Some parents are tired and too busy with their homemaking responsibilities. They find it hard to take the time needed to check their child's assignments carefully."

Students have more activities and options that compete for their time: jobs, sports activities, church choir, television, and family chores. Some teachers express concerns about students who perceive homework to be useless drudgery, as well as the lack of a stigma for those who fail to complete assignments.

More children today also have personal difficulties that are associated with a host of problems in school, including the ability to complete homework successfully. These include:

- troubled or unstable home lives;

- lack of positive adult role models;

- teenage pregnancies and parenting responsibilities;

- chemical dependency problems; or

- a high rate of mobility, found among families who move their children from school to school.

Overcoming the Obstacles

Fortunately, a number of strategies are known to help overcome the obstacles. Used together, these strategies can make homework less stressful, more enjoyable, and more meaningful. The tips can also help students master the ability to learn independently.

The information in this booklet is based on sound educational research and the experiences of award-winning teachers who have shared their favorite assignments and best strategies for getting students to complete homework successfully. These teachers come from all around the country and put their talents to work in many kinds of schools and communities—urban, inner-city, suburban, small town, and rural. They teach a broad range of subjects and at a variety of grade levels.

Echoing the sentiments of many of her colleagues, Barbara Allen, an Illinois high school art teacher, explains:

> "When students think of homework, usually it's a negative thought. But it shouldn't be, because learning should be fun. I don't think anybody today can become truly educated if they don't learn to work on their own."

Tips for Getting Homework Done

Lay out expectations early in the school year.

Before handing out the first homework assignment, go over the ground rules. A written explanation of the homework expectations increases chances that assignments will be completed successfully.

Let students know that:

 homework is important and has meaning; and

 doing assignments—or not doing assignments—has consequences, which may include lower grades if assignments go unfinished or undone.

All students need to be held to high standards; research shows that students make greater academic gains when teachers set and communicate high expectations to them.

Let students know how much and when homework will be assigned. Many teachers believe a consistent homework schedule helps students remember to do assignments—every Monday and Thursday night, for example. A consistent schedule can also help busy parents remember when their children's assignments are due.

Parents or other caregivers also need to understand the teacher's homework policy and expectations, particularly parents of younger students, who will be more actively involved in the assignments. All parents, however, need to know that their support and encouragement can be critical to the successful completion of assignments.

Teachers can communicate this information in many ways. Some teachers write notes home laying out their expectations, which parents or caregivers are asked to read, initial, and return. Some talk with parents about homework at back-to-school night. Some telephone parents and caregivers. Special efforts should be made to communicate with those who are hardest to reach.

- A Kentucky eighth-grade teacher of math, Mary Dunn, does two things every September to help her students complete math assignments successfully. First, she poses a question: "Do you want to pass?" She then tells them that if they want to do so they will have to complete their homework. Second, she makes consistent assignments. She tells them to expect a short assignment every night that they must take home, look at, and try to complete. "I demand a lot," she says. "I accept kids where they are, yet my standards and expectations are high—reachable, but high."

- At the start of each quarter, Jo Ann S. Harman asks students to sign a contract, which she believes improves the homework completion rate. As a part of the contract, this West Virginia teacher asks her junior high and high school French and English students to write down for her the grade they want for the 9-week grading period. She then asks them what grade they want for the semester, as well as the lowest grade with which they will be satisfied. She also asks students to write down what they need to do to achieve the goal, what they need to *stop* doing to achieve the goal, and how she can help them achieve their goal. Finally, students are asked to check one of the following two statements: "I am willing to change my habits to achieve my goal" or "I am *not* willing to change my habits to achieve my goal." Mrs. Harman urges students to set realistic goals. "Parents are glad to see that someone is urging their son or daughter to set goals and map out methods by which their goals can be met," she says. "This has brought about excellent results in the classroom. I can go back to the students if their grades are dropping and say, 'You and I don't want this.'"

- High school students in Cynthia Appold's visual arts/computer graphics classes also sign a contract with their teacher in which they spell out educational and personal goals for the year. The New York teacher asks her students to emphasize weak areas that interfere with their getting a good education. Homework expectations are a part of the contract. Parents review and initial the contract, making them as well as the students and teachers active participants in the students' education. Ms. Appold believes the contract builds trust among parents, students, and teachers—and makes it harder for students to ignore assignments.

- For the first few weeks of each school year, Rosemary Faucette calls one middle school student in each of her English classes each night to ask whether they have done their homework. If they say yes, the Arkansas teacher asks them to read it to her. If they say no, she asks when she can call back. "This takes time, but it is worth it," Ms. Faucette says. "They think you are the kind of teacher who will check." Word spreads quickly that she calls students at home. After the first few weeks of school, phone calls are no longer necessary—students know to buckle down and complete their assignments on time.

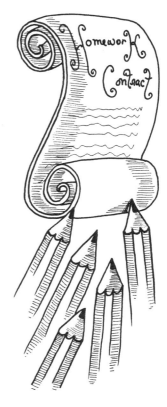

2 Create assignments with a purpose.

Any homework is *not* better than no homework at all. "The quality of an assignment makes a huge difference in whether it gets done," says Patricia Cygan, a high school social studies teacher from Washington. "Busywork is no good."

Homework can have several purposes. Ms. Blegen explains:

"We have to ask ourselves, 'What good does the homework do? What are we after?' I think it's only good if it's used for something that contributes to the class. Like getting ready for something, or finishing something, or polishing a presentation."

The major academic purposes of homework are to help children:

 review and practice what they have learned;

 get ready for the next day's class;

 learn to use resources, such as libraries, reference materials, and encyclopedias; and

 explore subjects more fully than time permits in the classroom.

In elementary school (and to a certain extent in junior high and high school) homework helps children develop good work habits and attitudes. It can:

 teach children the fundamentals of working independently; and

 encourage self-discipline and responsibility, as assignments provide some youngsters with their first chance to manage time and meet deadlines.

Homework is meant to be a positive experience and to encourage children to learn. Assignments should not be used as punishment.

Creating high-quality assignments with a purpose can be time-consuming. A high school history and social studies teacher from Wisconsin, Thomas J. Howe, explains:

"For much of the homework I assign, (students) know that the next day I will use it as the basis of a more meaningful whole. They know there is a purpose to what I'm assigning. They know the knowledge is crucial to the next day's activity. So the homework requires a fair amount of planning and thought as to why I'm giving it in the first place."

TIP

Make sure students understand the purpose.

Most students appreciate understanding the purpose of an assignment, but the purpose may not become evident until students are part way through an assignment or have completed it altogether.

- "I talk together with the kids about why an assignment is important," Ms. Blegen explains. "From the beginning, kids must know what you are after."

- "There is no confusion in my classroom—or little confusion—over the value of an assignment," says Mr. Howe. "I explain that when I assign it. I don't say: 'Read this; fill in the blank' without letting students know how it's important within the larger picture of what we are studying."

- Ms. Dunn uses Ken and Barbie dolls to help her eighth-grade math students learn math principles. Her students know before beginning an assignment what some of these principles are. But much of the assignment's significance does not become apparent until students have partially or fully completed it.

The Ken and Barbie assignment requires students to determine what the measurements of the dolls would be if they were life-sized people. Students also compare Barbie's measurements with a composite measurement drawn from all the girls in six of Ms. Dunn's eighth-grade math classes, and Ken's measurements with measurements from the eighth-grade boys. This assignment requires students to measure accurately and to analyze, as well as to design a spread sheet and read a bar graph. Information about volume, proportion, and ratio are also taught. And, not insignificantly, the assignment challenges image-conscious eighth-graders to rethink their notion of appropriate body size: Barbie's feet are so small that a real person, with comparable dimensions, wouldn't be able to walk.

Make assignments focused and clear.

Focused assignments are easier for students to understand and complete. Homework that tries to introduce or reinforce too many ideas is less likely to contribute to learning. This is particularly true for students whose abstract thinking hasn't developed to the point where they can integrate many concepts successfully.

• Most of Ken Boucher's homework assignments are distributed on half a sheet of paper. A full sheet can be intimidating, the elementary school music teacher from Maryland believes. Each assignment concentrates on one concept or issue—melodic components, for instance—and asks students to provide 4 or 5 examples. Mr. Boucher can easily tell from students' responses whether they have understood what he is trying to teach. If not, he can go back over the material.

• Providing a focus and the necessary background information is critical to having class discussions of assigned readings succeed, according to Ms. Faucette. Lacking a focus, she says, children often try to attack a reading all at once, "which ends up in frustration and chaos." The following assignment, however, provides the necessary focus: "Read Chapter 2 of *The Pearl* by John Steinbeck, concentrating on the behavior of Kino. Pick one important decisive action he took and explain what he would have to believe to act the way he did. Now advise Kino. Offer him alternative modes of behaviors. What would he have to believe to respond in the alternative manner you chose for him?"

TIP

5 Create assignments that challenge students to think and to integrate.

Homework can give students an opportunity to apply a concept beyond the controlled conditions of the classroom. It can also help students pull together and connect information from different places, sources, and subjects.

Good assignments often challenge students to break free of their usual way of thinking. Such assignments might require students to combine two ideas that are usually not associated.

Ms. Faucette suggests the following assignments for junior high students:

 Open a junk drawer and list 22 nouns for things you find there.

 Read the chapter on letter-writing. Then write a letter that breaks every single rule you know. "One hundred percent return on this one," she says: "How can you break the rule without knowing it?"

 Write a paragraph about your crazy Aunt Melba or Uncle Albert that breaks 10 rules of capitalization. The next day students present their paragraphs to see if their peers can figure out which rules were broken and correct them.

 Sit outside for 5 minutes and listen. Spend the next 5 minutes listing all the sounds you hear. Circle your favorite five. Write a poem about one.

 Write a 30-second radio spot using George Washington to sell deodorant soap. Work in four facts about his role as a general.

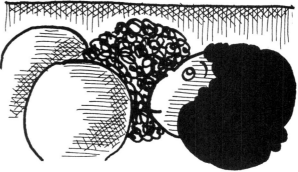

Generate 10 new classes for the school curriculum. Write a letter to school board members persuading them to implement one.

 Here is an answer: 54. Now generate 10 different questions, problems, or situations that can be answered with that number.

- Students in Fie Budzinsky's 11th-grade chemistry classes participate in "Chemistry on Stage," an assignment that integrates chemistry with theater, art, and writing. The Connecticut teacher instructs her students to research the life of a chemist who has made a significant contribution to his or her field. Students then write a script, which includes some aspect(s) of the chemist's life and a simulation of his or her scientific contributions. Students also design costumes, props, and sets and perform their 10- to 15-minute productions. Parents and students throughout the entire school are invited to attend, and food is served—always a draw for students. And Ms. Budzinsky says that, in addition to learning a lot, "Everybody has fun."

TIP

6 Vary assignments.

Students get bored if all assignments are similar. Try mixing approaches and styles. Since it's almost impossible for all assignments to interest all students, this approach increases the chances that all students will have some homework that they enjoy.

Short-term assignments can help students review and practice material that has already been covered in class. Math students may need to review decimals, for example, while students of foreign languages may be required to go over verb conjugations. Long-term projects give students a chance to vary the pace of their work, delve into subjects that interest them, integrate large amounts of information, and learn to manage their time and meet deadlines.

- Kit Bennett, an elementary school teacher in rural Idaho, explains, "I want assignments to peak their interest, to get them excited about their work. We do a bit of a drill. Sometimes it's just good old math or reading assignments they haven't finished in class. But I like to incorporate some creativity. So they might create a TV show or write a play."

- To help keep assignments fresh, a Florida math teacher, David E. Williams, asks his high school algebra students to make up their own equations—although he sets parameters. Students like this approach partly because they have helped create the homework assignment themselves.

- During his 38 years in the classroom, Montana teacher George Beyer learned the benefits of presenting material in new ways. Mr. Beyer wants his high school psychology students to learn key vocabulary words. His students were often bored or missed the main idea when he asked them to look up definitions. So he gives them the definitions, but has adopted two other techniques that allow them to learn the words.

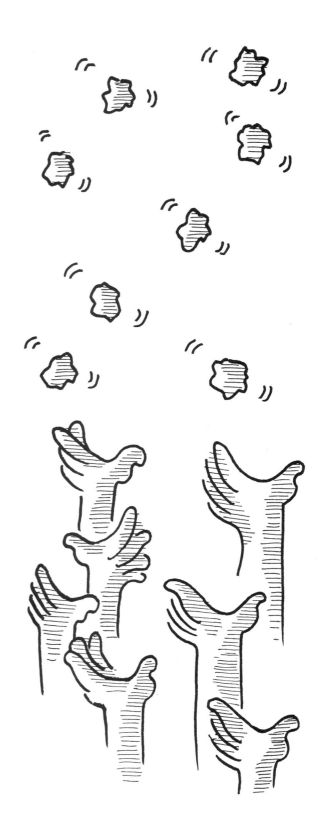

First, he gives one 'popcorn quiz' each semester—an idea he borrowed from his daughter, Carol Ward, who is also a Montana teacher. Before students arrive for class, Mr. Beyer writes each word on two separate pieces of paper. For a class of 30 students, 15 words will be written out, each one twice. Each student is given one sheet of paper, which he or she crumples up in a ball. When Mr. Beyer flashes the classroom lights, students toss their wadded paper into the air and catch another classmate's, repeating this 'popcorn' process until Mr. Beyer again flashes the lights about 30 seconds later. They have one additional minute to find one wad and match up with the classmate with the identical word, and another minute to write out the definition together. Students then come to the front of the classroom in pairs to read the word and definition. The pressure is on to learn the definitions, since everyone in the class gets the same grade—the number wrong subtracted from the total number of vocabulary words.

Second, Mr. Beyer surprises students at the classroom door with a vocabulary list of words he has asked them to learn. No one can get into the room before the tardy bell unless he or she gives a correct definition. "At first, they can't believe it—they have to *know* something just to get in!" Mr. Beyer says. "Later, it's fun to see their happy groans when they see me at the door." A variation—informing students ahead of time that all students who respond correctly to the word Mr. Beyer gives them at the classroom door the next day will be excused from the quiz and given 100 percent. "They work harder than normal just to miss the quiz," he says.

Variety can also invigorate teachers. Mrs. Harman is now in her 37th year of teaching English and French to 7th- through 12th-graders. "I rarely make the same writing assignment twice," she says. "Students deserve a fresh approach. And I try to teach one new book a year, so I'm not teaching the same things year after year."

TIP

7 Give homework that makes learning personal.

"The assignments that work best have to do with the students—the assignments are personal to them," explains Phyllis Orlicek, a high school English teacher from Arkansas. These assignments often allow students to draw upon their family, cultural, and community experiences and learn to appreciate better both their own and their classmates' backgrounds.

- Few, if any, projects that a Missouri teacher assigned to her seventh-grade social studies students packed as much punch as one involving heritage. Beth Reynolds' students heard excerpts read from Alex Haley's *Roots,* and they studied three cultural groups that influenced the United States: West Africans, Native Americans, and Renaissance Europeans. She also wanted her students to learn how immediate families and communities can affect what we know, believe, and do. So Ms. Reynolds asked her students to interview their parents to find out what three things they most wanted their children to know about life and why.

The results of this assignment, Ms. Reynolds says, "were beautiful—it gave parents and kids a time to get together and talk." Some parents composed letters to their children describing what they valued most—things like believing in oneself, doing one's best, having close family relationships, getting along with others, protecting the environment, and believing in God. The assignment, Ms. Reynolds says, "is one many of her students will not forget."

Tie assignments to the present.

Students often complain that they can't relate to assignments involving events that took place in the distant past.

An Ohio high school social studies teacher, Cathy Priest, explains:

> "Ancient history or American history are hard to teach unless you relate them to the present. It's hard to keep students interested and excited about events that happened 2000 or even 200 years ago, when they are not concerned about what happened 2 weeks ago."

- One Indiana teacher, Daniel Durbin, makes *Romeo and Juliet* more relevant to his high school literature students by discussing similarities between gangs today and in Shakespeare's time.

- A Louisiana social studies teacher, Ronald Cormier, helps his seventh and eighth-grade students learn about the Battle of Gettysburg by asking them to pretend to be contemporary television journalists, reporting live from the battlefield. In front of the class is a big cardboard box, cut out to resemble a television set. One student might do a "live interview" with General Lee, asking him if he had to second-guess himself what he'd do if the battle were his to fight again. Other students might interview other famous historical figures involved in this Civil War battle (or masquerade as the historical figures). Through these interviews, students learn specifics of the battle and gain perspective on its significance. Mr. Cormier serves as the anchorman who helps students pull together and integrate what they have learned.

 # Match assignments to the skills, interests, and needs of students.

Students are more apt to complete homework successfully when assignments:

 are neither too easy nor too hard;

 match a child's preferred learning style; and

 allow students to work on material that they truly enjoy.

Teachers with many students cannot be expected to customize all homework assignments for each student. However, most teachers can provide assignments to a heterogeneous class of students that vary in style, format, and content. This assures that all students have some that suit and interest them.

It is important to provide at-risk students with homework that challenges them to work to their full potential. A student may be at risk because of a variety of factors other than academic ability: for example, a student may be at risk because of Limited-English Proficiency (LEP), poverty, race, geographic location, or economic disadvantages.

An at-risk student could also be in an advanced placement class or a class for gifted and talented students.

Most teachers, however, give students in their advanced placement classes assignments that differ from those in non-a.p. classes. The assignments for honors class students are usually longer and require a level of abstract thinking that could frustrate less advanced students.

• Linda Fosnaught, a high school English teacher in Merrimack, New Hampshire, was frustrated with the number of her low-achieving students who were coming to class with their homework incomplete. So one day she stopped the class and told her students to complete the assignment right then and there. Those who had already done it were allowed to work ahead on other

homework or read ahead in their books. Without telling her students, Ms. Fosnaught timed how long it took for them to get the assignment done. Knowing how disappointed Ms. Fosnaught was, her students all worked efficiently and cooperatively. She then told her students that, although they had all been complaining about how much time her assignments took, that they had just managed to complete their work in seven minutes. She did not give them credit for the work they had just completed, but she pointed out to them that, had they taken this much time at home, they could have had full credit. Most of the class has been coming to class prepared ever since.

Teachers can also provide choices. Students may all be expected to master the same material, but they can do so in different ways. Providing choice increases the chances that students will enjoy more assignments. It also helps students feel they control parts of their learning, which enables some to enjoy an assignment more than they would otherwise.

- Mrs. Harman gave her junior high and high school English students broad leeway in a writing assignment involving time capsules. She asked her students to write something about their present lives that might intrigue their own children around the year 2040. "This is your opportunity to write for posterity!" Mrs. Harman told her students. Students could decide for themselves what to write and could choose their own format. Some wrote poetry. Some wrote journals. One sent her an e-mail message. One sent her a fax. One youngster wrote about his first-hand experiences as a visually impaired adolescent living in the 1990s. A senior accepted at the U.S. Naval Academy wrote on how he felt about beginning his military education.

TIP

10 Use school and community resources.

Many creative and rewarding homework assignments draw upon resources that are close at hand.

- Barbara Renoux teaches in a district with 2,100 students encompassing 88,000 square miles on the northern tip of Alaska. All of her 17 first- and second-grade students are Eskimos. In a community where, she says, "everyone is related to everyone" students respond particularly well to reading assignments that enable them to practice their developing skills on relatives and friends. So Ms. Renoux assigns a book or a poem that students are expected to read to their parents and to five other adults. Students collect signatures from each listener. "They love that," Ms. Renoux says. "They ask the janitor, the principal, their grandparents, and their cousins." Students with five signatures get a sticker on a classroom chart, which, she says, "they go for in a big way." At the end of the quarter, students with a certain number of stickers are allowed to camp out at the school, where they swim in the community pool and use the computer room.

- Jacqueline Omland sends her students to a nursery rhyme theme park near their home in Aberdeen, South Dakota, to apply their knowledge of trigonometry. The park's giant Jack-in-the-Beanstalk is too big for them to measure with a yardstick or tape measure. But they can view both the beanstalk and Jack and use their mathematical expertise to determine that they are approximately 80 feet and 7.5 feet tall respectively. The South Dakota teacher also uses an area playground to drive home basic elements of physics. Ms. Omland asks her students to determine how long it takes to slide down the playground slide wearing clothing made from various materials. She then asks them to time their slide with and without wax paper underneath them. The assignment also requires students to measure the length of the slide and its angle to learn about the coefficient of friction.

20

Match assignments to your style of teaching.

Assignments are more apt to succeed if the teacher is comfortable with them.

- One Nevada English teacher, Paula Naegle, tells the story of a fellow teacher who has discovered a way to boost her homework completion rate. But it might not suit a less athletically inclined teacher:

"She promises her students that if all of them have their homework on a given day, she will stand on her head or she will teach the class on her roller blades, or she will sing and dance for them. They actually do their homework, just to see if she will keep her word. And, by golly, she does. Somehow she wins them over early in the year with this stunt. She doesn't get 100 percent homework turned in for the rest of the year, but it really has made a difference."

TIP

12 Assign an appropriate amount of homework.

Many educators believe that homework is most effective for children in first through third grades when it does not exceed 20 minutes each school day. From fourth through sixth grades, many educators recommend from 20 to 40 minutes a school day for most students. For students in 7th- through 9th-grades, generally, up to 2 hours a school day is suitable. Ninety minutes to 2½ hours per night are appropriate for grades 10 through 12. Amounts that vary from these guidelines are fine for some students.

A common mistake, particularly among beginning teachers, is to assign too much homework. It can be hard to resist doing so if parents push for more homework and assume that the best teachers assign the most homework. (This is not necessarily the case.) Most often, however, a math teacher can tell after checking five algebraic equations whether students have mastered the necessary concepts.

- As Ms. Bennett explains, "Homework should not be overburdening. If there's too much, it becomes a drudgery. We need to keep [students'] attention—keep them inspired and wanting to do the homework. Otherwise, it's no good."

Teachers also need to coordinate their homework assignments with those of other teachers so that students aren't getting four assignments on a Tuesday night, but no assignments on Wednesday night. This coordination most often requires leadership and support from the principal or other administrator.

Finally, teachers need to keep alert to how long students take to complete assignments. It is natural in a class full of varied students for some to take longer than others. Moreover, it is fine that some students *do* take longer, since research shows that students with low test scores who spend substantial time on homework get grades as good as students with more ability who spend less time. If an assignment takes too long, however, this may signal that a student needs more instruction to complete it successfully.

TIP 13

Encourage and teach good study habits.

Children need good study skills in order to complete assignments successfully and gain the most from them academically. Unfortunately, many students haven't developed these skills, even by high school.

Some school districts provide comprehensive programs that spell out what study skills students in kindergarten through 12th-grade are expected to learn each year. This can help to assure that important skills are introduced early and nurtured throughout a student's years in school.

Kindergarten or first grade is not too early to introduce students to bringing work home, completing it, and returning it to school. Early assignments need to be simple. For example, very young students might be asked to bring a book for an adult to read to them—or for the child to read to an adult if he or she can do so. The adult might be asked to initial a bookmark indicating that the book has been read. These early assignments help students grasp the importance of learning at home and show adults that their support for homework is critical.

Older elementary school students are ready to learn more advanced study skills. These include:

 setting a regular time to study that fits in with the student's family schedule;

 removing distractions (turning off the television and discouraging social phone calls during homework time);

 gathering necessary supplies;

 recording assignments in an assignment book or on a calendar;

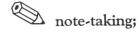 note-taking;

 managing time; and

 organizing for a test.

Students need to review these study skills in middle school and in junior high as their schedules become more complicated.

- "Not all seventh-graders are well organized," says Ms. Reynolds. "Some don't know how to handle having assignments from different teachers, or remember what they have to do and the books they need. So I spend lots of time on study skills. It would be nice if they had all of that down. But you can bat your head against the wall, or you can teach it." And once you do, she says, "They've got it."

- Reinforcing junior high school students' study skills can also reduce what Mr. Cormier describes as "the biggest problem for kids at this stage (seventh- and eighth-graders)—cramming."

Many students need to sharpen their study skills still further as they move into high school and find more demands being placed on their time. Many have trouble pacing themselves as they take on more extracurricular activities and accept part-time jobs.

- Richard Ruffalo, a New Jersey teacher, encourages his high school biology students to pace themselves by collecting a block of homework assignments at the same time. For example, he may make several assignments on one day, all of which are due 12 days later. Students quickly learn that the assignments must be completed in order to perform satisfactorily on tests given at the end of the 12 days—and that if they wait until the last minute to begin all of the assignments that their homework grades *and* test scores will suffer.

Students often imitate the organizing habits of important adults in their lives. Therefore teachers can set an example by being organized themselves. They can let students know that they, too, keep calendars to avoid forgetting things. And they can comment to students as they write down on their own calendar, "April 11—bring sombrero to school for Spanish class."

TIP

Provide constructive feedback.

Students are more apt to complete assignments and advance their learning when they get consistent and constructive feedback. Students need to know where they have excelled and where they need more work on an assignment. This conveys the vital message that homework helps students learn and is important.

Teachers can evaluate and review homework in a variety of ways. Many teachers give letter grades, others assign numbers, and many provide written comments. Grading homework motivates many students to do their best work and to learn more, but in some situations grades may not be beneficial. For example, written comments may be more constructive for a second-grade student whose homework assignment required her to write a poem.

Feedback is the most helpful when teachers provide specific suggestions on how the homework can be improved and discuss problems and remedies with individual students or the whole class. Math teachers may review a completed problem and point out any step in which an error has been made.

Peer feedback can also be helpful. In addition to providing students with another perspective of their work, peer feedback can help students learn cooperative social skills and teach students how to evaluate their own and other's efforts.

- A Kansas seventh-grade teacher, Christy McNally, explains, "I do not assign anything I don't grade and put a comment on, and the students know that. Anything I assign, I look at and record. So the students know they are doing something for a reason."

- The first thing students do when they walk in the door of Ms. Dunn's classroom is to place their homework on a stool in front of the class. While the eighth-grade math students are doing review exercises, Ms. Dunn looks through every paper. "I don't grade, but I look through

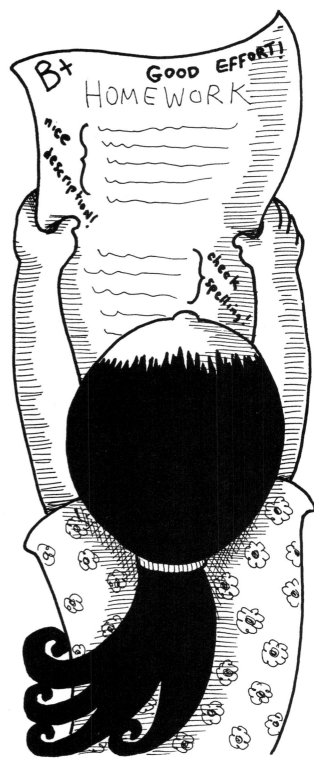

to make sure they have gotten the concept," she explains. "If everybody has left out #17, it was not clear. Then I can adjust the class and instruction accordingly."

- Mr. Howe reports receiving a higher return rate on homework since he began grading for both knowledge and skills and effort. "I think it makes a difference because it says to kids that making the effort has some real value that goes beyond the esoteric value of learning something," he says. "It says that when I put forth the effort, I will be rewarded in a tangible way."

- Mr. Beyer whizzes around the room for five minutes at the beginning of each class to glance at homework and see who has mastered the basic concepts. He grades some, but not all assignments and records his findings in his class book. At least every two weeks, students and their parents get a computer print-out showing their homework completion rate and their grades. "If any problems exist, I put in a note saying, 'How can I help you?'" he says. "In addition, I call their homes. In a small town, after teaching for 35 years, I've taught parents, their kids, their uncles and aunts. Word gets out that Beyer checks—and that he cares. That's the most important part."

TIP 15

Give praise and motivate.

Adults and children alike respond to praise. "Good first draft of your book report!" or "You've done a great job" can go a long way toward motivating students to complete assignments. Praise must be genuine. Children recognize insincere compliments.

● Competitions help motivate Ms. Orlicek's 12th-grade English students. She seeks local and national contests for individual students or the entire class to enter. The winners get their poems, essays, or short stories published or recognized. The competition motivates the students to write because they know they will have an audience other than the teacher.

● One Iowa teacher uses stickers and stamps to encourage her high school French students. Jill Olsen-Virlee distributes paper fleurs-de-lis each day to students who complete their homework. The fleurs (flowers), shaped like irises, are a symbol of royalty in France. Students also collect fleurs if they catch Ms. Virlee making a mistake—misspelling a word, for example, or forgetting an accent mark. "This keeps them sharp in class," she says. Students who collect enough fleurs can turn them in for French play money, which helps students master the country's monetary system.

● Ms. Allen motivates her high school art students by encouraging them to submit their best pieces for consideration in the school's permanent art collection. "It's a big deal," says Ms. Allen. "They get to leave a piece of themselves that will live at the school forever." In the three years since her Illinois high school began establishing this collection, 45 pieces have been selected. A range of individuals and institutions in Harrisburg sponsor the pieces and pay for their matting and framing and a plaque. Students whose pieces are selected by a committee of teachers, parents, and students have their art displayed at the school and get a picture in the local paper.

Give help as needed.

Students who don't understand an assignment need to know that help is available from the teacher or other appropriate person. Students at risk of academic failure or with personal difficulties may need extra support with both academic and logistical aspects of homework. It is important that they know it is okay to ask for help. In fact, it is imperative that they do so.

Teachers schedule time for students in a variety of ways. Some work with them before school. Some do so during free periods or part of the lunch period. Some give out their home phone numbers.

- Mr. Williams accepts calls at home up to 9:30 p.m. from his high school math students. Students who are embarrassed to call may do so anonymously. Most often, he talks through the problem with them to discover that they have missed some concept. He feels that by making himself available during the evening hours he saves time in class the next day.

- "Some kids come from families who give them no time to do anything at home except chores and babysitting younger siblings," reports Ms. Faucette. She asks these students to come in early in the morning or during their lunch periods to complete their homework in the classroom. "Sometimes they make it; sometimes not," she says. "What they learn, they learn in class, and I can't change that." Coming in before school or during lunch has an added benefit—it gives students a chance to talk with an adult.

In addition to teachers, students can get help from a range of other people and places:

 National Honor Society students serve as tutors in some schools.

 Homework hot lines have been established in many districts (reports on their effectiveness are mixed).

 "Study buddy" plans have been set up in some communities. These plans can be set up in a variety of ways. In some cases, students at a similar academic level are paired up. In other cases, the students might be at different levels, in which case the more advanced student serves as a tutor.

 Peer support helps many students wade through tough assignments. Ms. Dasenbrook asks her students to keep handy the telephone numbers of five students whom they can call to talk over homework problems.

 Study centers have been established in some school districts.

• Jean LaGrone teaches second-graders in a Nebraska school where more than 50 percent of the students receive free and reduced-price lunches. Some parents lack the skills and resources needed to support their children's homework efforts. So the district has funded a study center in a low-income apartment complex. A certified teacher is present after school to work with both children and parents. Kids can have a snack and receive whatever help and support they need to complete their homework. The books, computers, and supplies needed to complete assignments successfully are made available. The study center's teacher is given time each week to talk with the students' regular classroom teachers to keep them apprised of any problems.

Sometimes teachers can be a big help simply by alerting students to the repercussions for not doing an assignment.

• One Texas teacher, Ann Brock, talks with her third- and fourth-grade students if they don't hand in assignments. "If they don't do it, I ask them 'Why did you make that choice? Was it a good choice? Do you like what the outcome was?' They think things are done *to* them. They don't understand that what happens to them is a direct result of the choices they have made. I want them, if they make a bad choice, to see what they could do to change the outcome, so the next time they will make another choice." Ms. Brock believes that this process needs to begin when children are in about the first grade. "I think one of the big problems in schools is that nobody takes responsibility for their actions."

Communicate with parents.

Student learning improves when teachers communicate on a broad range of issues. Among the most vital of these is homework.

Parents are not expected to know or teach specific information to their children, particularly as their children get older. Parents can be an enormous help, however, in creating an environment at home that allows learning to take place. Teachers can also help create situations that allow parents and educators to work together to strengthen all learning, including what takes place at home.

Connecting with some parents can be a challenge. Many parents lead exceptionally busy lives. Some don't place as high a priority on homework as do teachers. The parents themselves may be in turmoil. Not all parents can help with homework to the extent that many teachers might hope.

Still, Ms. McNally explains, "When parents send us their child, they are sending us the very best they have, the very best child they could produce. They really care." The vast majority, she believes, "really want to help."

Teachers can do many things to improve communication:

 Contact parents early in the school year—before problems arise. Let them know you are available to talk about homework or any other aspect of their child's education. This information can be communicated at back-to-school nights, or at parent-teacher conferences scheduled for early in the school year. Telephone calls and notes home that must be signed and returned can also help convey this information.

Make a special effort to communicate with parents and caregivers who don't initiate contact with schools and teachers. Making these parents feel welcome in the school is the first step to improving communication. For example, communications can be improved by telephoning parents who don't come to parent-teacher conferences.

• Another U.S. Department of Education publication, *Reaching All Families,* outlines strategies that schools can use to reach out to all families and help involve them in their children's education.

 Tell parents how they can reach you, and when. Would you prefer that they telephone? Write a note? Set up a meeting with you? What hours would you prefer that they call? May they call you at certain times at home, or would you prefer that they do so at school?

• All students at Thomas Jefferson Middle School in Arlington, Virginia are given a homework assignment book on the first day of school. The book plays a central role in helping students get organized and complete assignments on time. The book also provides an easy and efficient way for parents and teachers to communicate with one another about assignments; if either has questions or concerns, they exchange notes in a special section included on each page. Teams of teachers also keep a telephone directory and log by each team phone. They contain addresses and parents' work and home phone numbers, as well as a record of conversations with parents, so that all team members know the number and nature of the calls. Some teachers also send home a unit guide before each new unit begins so that parents know what's coming and can ask their children appropriate questions.

 Tell parents about homework problems as soon as they arise. Parents are best able to work out a solution with the child and teacher if they know about the homework problem before report cards are distributed.

• "We have a real open-door policy," Ms. Bennett explains. "Parents are welcome at any time." Rolling out the welcome mat is a particular challenge since she teaches in a two-room school house in a strung-out ranching community. The school is 60 miles from the closest grocery store. However, Ms. Bennett says the school is "run like a family," and she tries to contact parents frequently with information about the good things their children are doing. "That way they will return my call when a problem comes up." she says. On the rare occasion when a homework problem becomes pesky, Ms. Bennett signs a contract with the parent and child that spells out how the problem is to be fixed. Notes also go back and forth from school to home so that communication lines are kept open. She also uses a monthly newsletter to parents to address any general problems, such as incomplete homework, that require their support.

 Tell parents and caregivers how you want them to be involved with homework. Different teachers have different expectations, which can confuse parents. The parents' involvement will need to change as students mature and can assume more responsibility.

Below are ways you might suggest parents be involved. For example, they can:

 Set a regular time for homework—one that works for their child and their family. Research shows a correlation between successful students and parents who create and maintain family routines.

Pick a fairly quiet study area with lots of light and supplies close by. A desk in the bedroom is nice, but for many youngsters the kitchen table or a corner of the living room works just fine.

 Remove distractions. Turn off the television and discourage social telephone calls during homework time.

 Provide supplies and resources such as pencils, pens, erasers, writing paper, an assignment book, and a dictionary.

 Provide aids to good organization, such as an assignment calendar, book bag, and folders.

 Encourage parents to check with you, the school counselor, or the principal if they cannot provide their child with the necessary supplies and resources.

 Look over the homework, but do not do the homework for them.

 Review teacher comments on homework that has been returned and discuss with their child.

 Contact the teacher if there's a homework problem or need they cannot resolve. Teachers may need to be flexible in scheduling meetings with parents to discuss homework problems in order to accommodate inflexible job schedules and other demands.

Provide parents with a list of questions to ask their child:

 What's your assignment today?

 Is the assignment clear?

 When is it due?

 Do you need special resources (e.g., a trip to the library or access to a computer)?

 Do you need special supplies (e.g., graph paper or posterboard)?

 Have you started today's assignment? Finished it?

 Is it a long-term assignment (e.g., a term paper or science project)?

 For a major project, would it help to write out the steps or make a schedule?

 Would a practice test be useful?

Encourage parents to monitor television-viewing and select with their children the programs they may watch. Inform parents that more then two to three hours of television-viewing on school nights is related to lower student achievement. Moderate television viewing, especially when supervised by parents, can help children learn.

- Ms. Faucette asked her junior high English students to give up television for one week as part of their study on television and media values. Those who succeeded were rewarded with 40 extra credit points and a pizza party (they bought). Every day they wrote in journals, held class debriefing sessions, talked about how hard it was to give up television and generated lists of alternative things to do, including homework. During this week, not one student failed to turn in homework, compared with the usual 80 to 85 percent completion rate. "When I asked them why (more were completing assignments), they frankly admitted, 'We have nothing else to do.' TV sucks time away from these kids."

If problems with homework arise, work out a solution together with the parent(s) and the child. The strategy will depend on what the problem is, how severe it is, and the needs of the student. For example:

Is the homework too hard? Perhaps the child has fallen behind and will need extra help from the teacher, parent, or tutor to catch up.

 Does the child need to make up a lot of work because of absences? The first step might be working out a schedule with the teacher.

 Has the child been diagnosed with a learning disability or is one suspected? If so, the child may need extra help and the teacher may need to adjust some assignments.

 Does the child need extra support, beyond what home and school can give? A mentor program in the community might be able to provide it, with the child being paired with an adult volunteer who can help with the youngster's special needs. Many good mentor programs operate in schools, universities, community organizations, churches, and businesses.

In resolving homework problems, make sure communication is clear. End a meeting with a parent only after you are sure that everyone understands the strategy planned to ease the problem. Follow up to make sure that the approach you agreed to is working.

Show respect for students.

Students are more inclined to complete assignments when teachers and students respect one another. Students sense when teachers care about them and want them to do their best work.

- "I really talk to my kids," says Ms. Budzinsky. "I'm very, very close to my students. I know them personally. Kids will do things for you if they know you respect them as people, as real people, and not just as students—that you care about them as human beings. By the second day of class, I have all my students' names memorized. This is important. As a result of this, I think kids will do more homework. Half the reason they do the homework is because they like me. It's not always because they realize it's in their best interest."

- "If students know you really care about how they do, if they know the teacher likes and cares about them, they are going to try harder," says Mr. Ruffalo. Toward that end, he talks privately with any student who isn't doing well—and who isn't completing homework assignments. "Screaming and yelling doesn't work," Mr. Ruffalo explains. "I reason. I tell them why it's important to do well. I say, 'Look. Your family really wants you to do well.' I tell them, 'If you want to support a family and have a nice lifestyle, you need a good job with benefits. For all those things you'll need an education. Education is the key that unlocks the shackles of poverty.'"

- Ms. Olsen-Virlee tells students that they can negotiate to change when an assignment is due if something major intervenes—for example, a major sporting event in which they want to participate. "I don't always back off," she says. "Sometimes I challenge why they can't get [the assignment] done." But the fact that students know she is willing to take their needs into consideration sets a tone of respect that reverberates throughout her classroom.

Students sense when teachers are committed to their learning and view it as valuable for both students and teachers alike.

- A New Hampshire teacher, Deborah Woelflein, keeps a journal of her own whenever she asks her ninth-grade English students to make entries in theirs. Then if, as often happens, some of her students are reluctant to share thoughts or ideas from their own journals, she'll start by sharing her entries. The same approach works well with older students, she says. "I'll say, 'Take a look at this—tell me what I should work on.' Then they'll criticize mine—they'll say, 'I don't think this sentence sounds right. I don't think your introduction is clear. Here's another example you could put in.' This helps them see learning as a two-way thing. The teacher is learning at the same time they are. They see that it is worthwhile to do the work and get feedback from others. The more able students see that the assignment is not just busywork."

Conclusion

Homework can bring together children, parents, and teachers in a common effort to improving student learning. Teachers are a vital link in making this happen.

The benefits of homework begin in school. Students who complete their homework successfully improve their chances for academic success. But homework develops habits and attitudes that work to a student's advantage far beyond the classroom. Qualities like self-discipline, responsibility, and a love of learning benefit students throughout their lives.

References

Butler, Jocelyn A., (1987). "*Homework.*" Published as part of School Improvement Research Series by Northwest Regional Educational Laboratory, Portland, Oregon. (November).

Chavkin, Nancy, Editor, (1993). *Families and Schools in a Pluralistic Society.* Albany, New York: SUNY Press.

Clark, Faith, and Clark, Cecil, with Marta Vogel, (1989). *Hassle-free Homework.* New York, New York: Doubleday.

Cooper, Harris, (1989). *Homework.* White Plains, New York: Longman, Inc.

Corno, Lyn, "Homework is a Complicated Thing," in *Educational Researcher,* Vol. 25, No. 8, (November 1996) pp. 27-39.

Doyle, Mary Anne E., and Barber, Betsy S., *Homework as a Learning Experience,* Third Edition, (1990), Washington, D.C.: National Education Association publication.

English, David A., and Flatley, Joannis K., (1985). *Homework—And Why* (PDK Fastback No. 218). Bloomington, Indiana: Phi Delta Kappa Educational Foundation.

Epstein, Joyce L., "Homework Practices, Achievements, and Behaviors of Elementary School Students." ERIC *Digest,* (1983), ED 250351.

Featherstone, Helen, "Homework" in *The Harvard Education Letter*, Vol. 1, No. 1. (February 1985).

Keith, Timothy Z. "Time Spent on Homework and High School Grades: A Large-Sample Path Analysis." *Journal of Educational Psychology*, Vol. 74, No. 2, (1982), pp. 248-253.

Keith, Timothy Z., Reimers, Thomas M., Fehrmann, Paul G., Pottebaum, Sheila M., and Aubey, Linda W. "Parental Involvement, Homework, and TV Time: Direct and Indirect Effects on High School Achievement." *Journal of Educational Psychology*, Vol. 78, No. 5 (1986), pp. 373-80.

Moles, Oliver C., and D'Angelo, Diane. "Homework and Home Learning Activities" in *Building School-Family Partnerships for Learning: Workshops for Urban Educators.* U.S. Department of Education ERIC Document #364-651 (September 1993).

Moles, Oliver, (1996). *Reaching All Families: Creating Family-Friendly Schools.* Produced in collaboration with the Partnership for Family Involvement in Education and the U.S. Department of Education.

Paulu, Nancy, and Perkinson, Kathy, (1995). *Helping Your Child with Homework*, Washington, D.C.: U.S. Department of Education.

Radencich, Marguerite C., and Schumm, Jeanne Shay, (1988). *How to Help Your Child With Homework*, Minneapolis, Minnesota: Free Spirit Publishing Inc.

U.S. Department of Education, *Strong Families, Strong Schools: Building Community Partnerships for Learning*. Washington, D.C.: U.S. Department of Education. (September 1994).

U.S. Department of Education, (1987). *What Works: Research about Teaching and Learning*, Washington, D.C.: U.S. Department of Education.

Wahlberg, H.J. "Homework's Powerful Effects on Learning." *Educational Leadership*, Vol 42, No. 7, pp. (April 1985) 76-79.

Resources

American Federation of Teachers, (1991). *Home Team Learning Activities for the Early Grades.*[*]

Canter, Lee, and Hauser, Lee, (1987). *Homework Without Tears.* New York: Perennial Library.

Eisenberg, Michael B., and Berkowitz, Robert E., (1996). *Helping with Homework: A Parent's Guide to Information Problem-Solving.* Syracuse University: ERIC Clearinghouse on Information and Technology.

Epstein, Joyce L., Salinas, Karen C., and Jackson, Vivian, (1994, revised). *Manual for Teachers: Teachers Involve Parents in Schoolwork (TIPS) Language Arts, Science/Health, and Math Interactive Homework in the Middle Grades.* Also, Prototype Activities for TIPS Language Arts, Science/Health, and Math (260 sample homework assignments) for grades 6, 7, 8. Baltimore, Maryland: Center on School, Family, and Community Partnerships.

Epstein, Joyce L., and Salinas, Karen C., (1992). *Manual for Teachers: Teachers Involve Parents in Schoolwork (TIPS) Math and Science Interactive Homework in the Elementary Grades.* Also, prototype homework activities for TIPS Math (K-5) and Science (3).

Epstein, Joyce L., Coates, Lucretia, Salinas, Karen C., Sanders, Mavis G. and Simon, Beth.S., (1997). *School, Family, and Community Partnerships: Your Handbook for Action.* Thousand Oaks, California: Corwin Press.

Klavan, Ellen, (1992). *Taming the Homework Monster.* New York: Poseidon Press.

Moles, Oliver, (1996). *Reaching All Families: Creating Family-Friendly Schools.* Produced in collaboration with the Partnership for Family Involvement in Education and the U.S. Department of Education.

The National PTA and the National Education Association, (1995). *Helping Your Students Get the Most Out of Homework.*[**]

Paulu, Nancy, and Perkinson, Kathy, (1995). *Helping Your Child with Homework.* Washington, D.C.: U.S. Department of Education.

Rich, Dorothy, (1988, 1992). *Megaskills: How Families Can Help Children Succeed in School and Beyond.* Boston: Houghton Mifflin Company.

Sanders, M.G., (November, 1996). "Building Family Partnerships that Last" in *Educational Leadership,* Vol. 54, No. 3, pp. 61-66.

Sonna, Linda Agler (1990). *The Homework Solution: Getting Kids To Do Their Homework.* Charlotte, Vermont: Williamson Publishing Co.

---

[*]English and Spanish versions available free in limited quantities by writing: AFT Public Affairs Department, 555 New Jersey Avenue, NW, Washington, DC 20001.

[**]This document is available on the National PTA's website at http://www.PTA.org

Invaluable information to guide teaching and homework is available on the internet. Because the resources are constantly changing and expanding, it is not possible to provide a complete list of all sites that might be helpful. However, below are a few good places to look for information:

- http://www.ed.gov/

- http://www.teachnet.com

- http://www.refdesk.com/

- http://www.studyweb.com/

- http://inet.ed.gov/~dtimm/teachers/teacher2.htm

- http://www.askanexpert.com/askanexpert

- http://www.askeric.org/Qa/Toolbox/

Acknowledgments

Thank you to the many people and organizations who contributed to the creation and production of *Helping Your Students With Homework: A Guide for Teachers.*

The National Teacher of the Year Program provided names of state and national teachers of the year who contributed information and participated in extensive conversations. They include: Barbara Allen from Illinois, Cynthia Appold from New York, Kit Bennett from Idaho, George Beyer from Montana, Mary Beth Blegen from Minnesota, Ann Brock from Texas, Fie Budzinsky from Connecticut, Ronald Cormier from Louisiana, Patricia Cygan from Washington, Mary Elizabeth Dunn from Kentucky, Daniel Durbin from Indiana, Rosemary Faucette from Arkansas, Javier Gonzalez from California, Jo Ann S. Harman from West Virginia, Ray Hasart from Oregon, Thomas Howe from Wisconsin, Jean LaGrone from Nebraska, Paula Naegle from Nevada, Christy McNally from Kansas, Jill Olsen-Virlee from Iowa, Jacqueline Omland from South Dakota, Phyllis Orlicek from Arkansas, Catherine Pittman from Georgia, Cathy Priest from Ohio, Beth Reynolds from Missouri, Barbara Renoux from Alaska, Susan Rodriguez from Pennsylvania, Richard Ruffalo from New Jersey, David Williams from Florida, and Deborah Woelflein from New Hampshire.

Other teachers who contributed information include: Anne Bogardt from California, Ken Boucher from Maryland, Diane Coggins from Virginia, Eleanor Dasenbrook from Virginia, Linda Fosnaught from New Hampshire, Joyce Higginbotham from Washington, D.C., Andrea Myers from Virginia, and Carol Ward from Montana.

Other educators who reviewed drafts and contributed their expertise and experiences include: Laura Altamar, Annette Anderson, Joyce Epstein, Randy Hollister, Jan Jaffke, Sharon Jones, Bob McClure, Molly Merry, and Joan Snowden.

Within the U.S. Department of Education, a special thank you to Phil Carr, Maura Daly, Blane Dessy, Gerald Devlin, Cynthia Dorfman, Terry Dozier, Lance Ferderer, Patty Hobbs, Ellen Holland, Robert LeGrand, Ollie Moles, Kathryn Perkinson, Joan Trumble, and Barbara Vespucci.

Helping Your Students With Homework was prepared under the direction of Sharon Bobbitt, Director of the Office of Educational Research and Improvement's Office of Reform Assistance and Dissemination (ORAD), Ronald Cartwright, and Peirce Hammond, director of ORAD. A special thanks to the editor, Linda Darby, and the illustrator, Margaret Scott.

ISBN 0-16-049436-2